National Academy of Design

Seasons at The New Yorker
Six Decades of Cover Art

New York June 1 - July 31, 1984

Published by United Technologies Corporation

Designed by Derek Birdsall and produced by Birdsall & Co.
Typeset in Monophoto Van Dijck, 203
Printed and bound in Great Britain by Balding + Mansell Limited on Basingwerk Parchment and Parilux Matt paper using Inmont printing inks.

New Yorker covers have been captivating readers
for years. I am pleased United Technologies could help
present this celebration of *New Yorker* cover art.

Harry J. Gray
Chairman and Chief Executive Officer
United Technologies Corporation

Introduction

The National Academy of Design takes great pleasure in offering this sampling of eighty drawings and paintings, each of which was chosen at one time or another by *The New Yorker's* editorial staff as the magazine's weekly cover image. Taking the calendar year as a thematic focus, we have assembled these works with several goals in mind: to gather for the first time since 1946 a selection of *The New Yorker's* most striking cover images, now spanning its fifty-nine year history; to capture the evolution in style and concept of these illustrations; and to honor many gifted artists whose talents in the graphic arts have perhaps received inadequate recognition.

These works for the exhibition were chosen from more than three thousand issues, the tear sheets of which are meticulously filed in *The New Yorker's* library. Credit for this monumental surveying and selection goes to Dita Amory, cataloguer of drawings and prints at the National Academy of Design. Winnowing the supply of cover images to a small number was no easy task. Understandably, some covers did not suit the seasonal content of the exhibition. For others, there was no record of ownership. Regrettably, some of the original art work was simply inaccessible. (One artist wrote from France that his cover drawings were buried in a warehouse in New Jersey, and there was thus no hope of their exhibition.)

Apart from a few disappointments, we have been extraordinarily lucky in locating so many of our favorites. The exhibition would not have materialized had it not been for the support and enthusiasm of many lenders, a considerable number of whom are the cover artists themselves. You will note familiar signatures, some better known in the repertoire of cartoon art than in that of cover imagery. We also wish to acknowledge the creative and financial support provided by United Technologies Corporation in the production of this catalogue and also its interest and support of the exhibition. In all, we hope you will have as much enjoyment from this exhibition and catalogue as we have had from the research and organization of the show.

JOHN H. DOBKIN
Director
National Academy of Design

Lenders

Charles Addams

Constantin Alajalov

Patricia Arno

Peter Barlow

Andreas Bartsch, Munich

Barbara Bemelmans

Rosamond Berg

Mrs. Abe Birnbaum

Judith W. Brown

Mr. and Mrs. John Chancellor

Mr. and Mrs. D. M. Collins Jr.

Susan Davis

Robert Day

Rudolf Ensmann, Munich

Mr. and Mrs. Peter F. Fleischmann

Tom Funk

Galerie Bartsch & Chariau, Munich

Galerie St. Etienne, New York

Mr. and Mrs. James Geraghty Jr.

Mr. and Mrs. Henry J. Goldschmidt

Harry's Bar, London

Suzanne Funk Holland

John Locke Studios, Inc., New York

Joyce Golden & Associates, Inc., New York

Edward Koren

Anatol Kovarsky

Robert Kraus

Lakeview Museum of Arts and Sciences, Peoria, Illinois

Library of Congress, Washington, D.C.

Donald A. Macrae

Manufacturers Hanover Trust Company, New York

Charles Martin

Dr. and Mrs. Francis D. Moore

The New Yorker Magazine, Inc.

Nicholls Gallery, New York

Mrs. Tyson Nimick

The Pace Gallery, New York

Carola Portas

Edith Quintana

Joellen Rapée

Stewart Read

Mrs. Nelson A. Rockefeller

Samuel and June Rosenfeld

Charles Saxon

Rachel Scott

Dr. and Mrs. Robert T. Sessions

Deborah Jane Sheridan

James Stevenson

Syracuse University Art Collections

Mr. and Mrs. R. J. Trane

William Zinsser

and Private Collections

Acknowledgements

The National Academy of Design gratefully acknowledges the coöperation and participation of the many who have lent their time and expertise to this exhibition. Without the support of *The New Yorker's* staff, both editorial and business, the exhibition would remain but a dream. We wish to thank the art editor, Lee Lorenz, and his assistant, Anne Hall, for kindly locating the owners of several drawings. Helen Stark, *The New Yorker's* librarian, graciously shared her resources with us in the preliminary selection process. Particular thanks are also due Hoyt Spelman and Joyce Richter. Luis Dominguez coördinated publication efforts from the magazine's London office. Marie Dalton-Meyer and Christine Rothenberg, of United Technologies, have patiently lent support and advice, masterminding this exhibition catalogue throughout its production. Barbara Nicholls, of the Nicholls Gallery, was extraordinarily helpful. She identified the ownership of many drawings and paintings, often paving our way with artists and friends. To her, we owe a singular debt of gratitude. The staff of the museum has been supportive since the project's inception. Nancy Krieg, our conservator, and Beth Harrington and Andrew Blume, volunteers in the Department of Drawings and Prints, deserve special mention. Betsy Arvidson coördinated deliveries, telephone calls, and other communications with characteristic ease. Finally, it is to the lenders that we owe a special thanks. From London to Munich, from Key Biscayne, Florida, to Amherst, New Hampshire, every lender has expressed enthusiasm for the project, an immediate willingness to contribute art work (in many cases denuding walls), and satisfaction in taking part in this much anticipated retrospective exhibition of *New Yorker* cover art.

DITA AMORY
Department of Drawings and Prints
National Academy of Design

A morning light

Having been founded in 1925, *The New Yorker* has attained what is considered a great age for a magazine. When Harold W. Ross, its only begetter and first editor, died, in 1952, he was succeeded by William Shawn, who continues to preside over its contents with the iron will and gentle demeanor that once led a contributor, Harold Brodkey, to describe him as combining the best attributes of Napoleon and St. Francis of Assisi. As the decades pass, some readers, intending to pay the magazine a compliment, pay it what amounts to an insult instead: they congratulate *The New Yorker* on being the very thing that it isn't and wouldn't wish to be; to wit, a publication that remains unaltered by time, immaculately faithful to its beginnings.

What tiresome nonsense this is! I have been writing for the magazine for upward of half a century, and I swear that I can observe it changing continuously – almost from one issue to the next, and certainly from one year to the next. Its purported sameness is largely an optical illusion. Because the physical layout of the magazine has changed so little over its lifetime, what one holds in one's hands is indeed a familiar presence; one perceives from week to week that it is roughly the same size as ever, with the same typography and the same department headings. (Some of the headings have grown quaint with age; Pauline Kael writes about movies under "The Current Cinema," but I doubt if the word "cinema" has ever crossed her lips, except in mockery and preceded by a robust Anglo-Saxon modifier.) The optical illusion I speak of is much heightened by the fact that, though the nature of the editorial matter may change, it is to be found embedded in advertisements of an invariable sleekness and seductiveness, repeating over the generations a single subliminal exhortation, "Spend! Spend! Spend!"

This optical illusion becomes, through repetition, a psychological reality. All of us are contented victims of the habitual; salivating at the least ringing of the tiniest bell, we tend to resent whatever is novel, or perhaps only unexpected, in the course of our lives. By long custom, *The New Yorker* publishes some twenty cartoons a week, and it is to these cartoons that our subscribers are likely to turn first; afterward, there may be time for them to read The Talk of the Town, a short story or two, and even a few of the departments. To my chagrin (I may just mention in passing), I know nothing about the readers of the Theatre department, the writing of which I share with my colleague Edith Oliver, except what I learn from letters they occasionally address to me. From these letters I deduce that they believe me to be short and fat (I am not), and that they are grateful to me not for my perspicacity but for my writing briefly (that I do).

Would our subscribers notice if the number of cartoons we publish weekly were to drop off from twenty to twelve or fifteen? I suspect that the difference would make them uneasy but they would be unable to pinpoint the source of their uneasiness. Once upon a time, James Geraghty, who served as art editor before the incumbent, Lee Lorenz, complained to me that he had far too many talking-animal jokes "on the bank," which is an office term for work that is ready for immediate publication. I suggested that he fill an entire issue of the magazine with talking animals, to see if anyone would notice. He accepted my suggestion, the cartoons appeared, and no one noticed. Or it may be that they noticed and out of kindness chose not to call attention to what could only have been our professional inattentiveness. But kindness is not a commonplace among our keen-eyed readers; they rejoice to catch us out in even the most infinitesimal errors – including typographical errors, of which we have, in these increasingly aberrant high-tech times, as many as one or two a year.

The New Yorker's covers play a major role in the optical illusion I have been discussing. Week in and week out, whether on newsstands or in the mail, they provide us with that welcome shock of recognition which we feel on encountering any old friend; the times may be aberrant, but here, we feel, is stability, here is reassurance. And yet not so fast! The New Yorker's covers are as subject to change as The New Yorker's text, though the changes, when they occur, are less conspicuous, the artist's hand being, to my mind, nearly always more subtle – and more subtly prankish – than the hand of the writer. That distinction aside, and to clear the ground, I ought to state at once that there is, in any event, no such thing as a New Yorker cover, as there is no such thing as a New Yorker short story (though many of our readers are quick to claim that there is, apparently seeing little difference between short stories by John Updike, Donald Barthelme, Alice Adams, and Laurie Colwin). From the beginning, the magazine has taken pride in the variety of modes of expression available to its artists and writers; if these modes have seemed to demonstrate more collusion than collision, that is because the number of people who choose the contents of the magazine is remarkably small and they share, not unremarkably, a similar taste.

If one cannot say that there is such a thing as a New Yorker cover, one can at least say that there are three or four types of art work that appear with considerable frequency on the covers of The New Yorker: those that are purely decorative, those that are topical or seasonal, and those that contain a mild satiric swipe or possibly a small, covert joke. Our first art editor, Rea Irvin, fancied decorative covers, bold in line and color and not necessarily having much of anything to do with the magazine. Indeed, our very first cover depicted a Regency fop, who eventually came to bear the name of Eustace Tilley, and who was ideally unsuitable in almost every way for the magazine that Ross had in mind – a magazine that he said wasn't to be published for the likes of an old lady in Dubuque. The implication was that the magazine would be vigorous, iconoclastic, and perhaps unmannerly, which is to say that it would be all the things that Irvin's fop, elegantly observing through a monocle an insubstantial butterfly, was not. Why on earth Ross permitted Irvin to impose such a cover on him I have no idea. Maybe he was in awe of him, as in his early years he was in awe of many successful people, thinking of them as lucky insiders, because he himself was so obviously an outsider — a high school dropout from far-off Aspen, then a long-forgotten ghost town in the Rockies.

Topical covers have to do with certain recurrent events, which go on being celebrated down the years — political conventions and such holidays as Christmas, St. Valentine's Day, Halloween, and Thanksgiving. (I remember with particular pleasure an enormous Halloween pumpkin by Abe Birnbaum, its gorgeous orange hue filling the cover from top to bottom.) Decade after decade, we rejoice in covers that salute the changing of the seasons — a winter twilight, a summer cottage open to blue sea and golden sand, a maple dropping its fiery autumn leaves beside the Housatonic, the first springtime hyacinth. In the old days — and I take care not to say the good old days — there were more covers with jokes than there are today; Peter Arno, in particular, liked to draw covers that illustrated a comic mishap of some kind — much as Rowlandson might have drawn a similar mishap a couple of centuries earlier, though he would have employed far less vivid colors than those that Arno favored.

In the almost sixty years of the magazine's existence, so many hundreds of cover artists, so many thousands of covers! It is in the nature of things that a number of the most distinguished of these artists are long since dead and, I fear, forgotten, or beginning to be forgotten. Who now, especially among our younger readers, is likely to remember Will Cotton, Helen Hokinson, Garrett Price, Ludwig Bemelmans, Mary Petty, Ilonka Karasz, Edna Eicke? We have reason to be grateful that they are being brought back to us on this occasion, and not merely in the form in which we first encountered them, as printed covers, but in the lustre and tenderness of the original work, seemingly fresh from the artist's hand. Freshness has always been a characteristic of *The New Yorker* at its best; it is an attribute hard to husband and so in constant jeopardy. Henry James described growing old as a slow, reluctant march into the enemy country — the country of general lost freshness. It strikes me that *The New Yorker*, for all its formidable age, has not yet crossed the borders of that country. A morning light falls slantwise across our covers. In their still air trembles the promise of something that is just about to happen. And it is something that we sense will make us happy.

— BRENDAN GILL

A special moment, fleetingly observed

James Geraghty, who was the art editor of *The New Yorker* for more than three decades, was once asked to define the qualities of a *New Yorker* cover. After long consideration, he arrived at an illumination. "A *New Yorker* cover," he said, "is something I like." His quip masked a fundamental truth. Unlike other publications, which tend to become bogged down in research and commercial considerations, *New Yorker* covers — and, indeed, all the editorial content of the magazine — are and always have been simply the results of what the editors like. From the selections of Harold Ross, and Geraghty, to those of William Shawn, and Lee Lorenz, the present art editor, the covers defy definition. Artists are invited to submit their work. Nothing is assigned, nothing is directed. The work is welcomed or it is not.

I don't mean to imply that changes or revisions are not suggested, but basically the covers are the private inspirations of the artists. Though Harold Ross, the originator of the magazine and self-declared philistine who rode herd on the creative flock, was anything but inarticulate, his scribbled criticisms of drawings were usually minimal — like his famous notation "Make better." According to Geraghty, he was particularly shy about suggesting changes on covers. When Geraghty was brand-new in the job, Ross craftily used him to suggest a change in a cover by Ludwig Bemelmans — something that Ross had never dared to do himself. Geraghty innocently began, "Mr. Bemelmans, we think you might just change — " He never finished. Bemelmans, with a beatific smile, said, "That's all right, Jimmy," took the cover, tore it in half, and walked out.

These days, most of the cover artists accept normal editing, but the concept and the performance remain their own. I have had the good fortune to work with both Geraghty and Lorenz, bringing my drawings and covers to the shabby twentieth-floor offices of the art department on so many Tuesday mornings that the familiar ritual has become the weekly high tide of my life. Lorenz, a masterly cartoonist himself, communicates easily with the artists on their terms. Geraghty was more like Ross. I remember him looking at my pictures, rubbing his hand across his jaw, looking up at the ceiling, then back at the picture. Finally, he'd clear his throat. "May I say something?" he'd ask. "Why, yes," I'd say. Geraghty knew perfectly well that I had just driven forty-five miles from Connecticut for the express purpose of having him say something. There would follow a series of unintelligible grunts, a finger jabbing at the drawing. Sentences would be begun and aborted. I'd find myself offering possible areas for revision to cover his silences, and soon we'd arrive at the kind of change he refused to initiate himself. As differently as Lorenz and Geraghty dealt with this customary dialogue, the results were the same: the artists solved the problems.

I think that the person who has come closest to defining a *New Yorker* cover is William Steig. Referring to the classic Japanese poetic form, he said, "For me, a cover is a moment of *Haiku* – a special moment, fleetingly observed." I know that Lee Lorenz warms to this perception, too, and I keep it in mind always.

I asked Lorenz for a definition, but he demurred. "A definition is a kind of obituary," he said. "Our covers are what our artists bring us, and I don't want them to feel limited by what we've published in the past or by my vision of the future. I remember when I first saw Gretchen Simpson's portfolio. Everything that's special in her work was there, but she was using her talent to create what she imagined were '*New Yorker* covers.' They were a kind of anthology of what we had published over the previous few years. I asked her to come in and discuss her work. I suggested that she show us work that was meaningful to her rather than try to shape her work to suit us. She did, and, as a result, gave us covers that moved in a whole new direction. That sort of thing doesn't happen if one imposes one's expectations on the artist."

Lorenz continued, "*The New Yorker* is a magazine to be kept at home and read at leisure, and I think of our covers as pleasurable additions to one's living room rather than as newsstand pitchmen. Although some covers have been successfully transformed into posters, they seem to me a more intimate kind of art form. Something to turn to in quiet moments and enjoy at arm's length."

Lorenz was referring obliquely to the objection sometimes heard that the name of the magazine isn't always easy to find in the clutter of newsstand displays. The answer is that those who are looking for it find it. But, bold or delicate, the covers are designed, like posters, with the logotype an integral part of the whole. The choosing of colors for the lettering and the identifying sidebar on the left is a special art in itself.

Looking at the list of artists represented in this collection, and their work, spanning almost sixty years, I'm dazzled by the variety of concepts and the constant surprises in each artist's contribution to the image of this one magazine. Many, like Arno, Addams, Steig, Birnbaum, and Getz, have done hundreds, and the list includes artists who have been associated with the magazine from the beginning and are still producing work with the same freshness and excitement.

All these artists share one characteristic: They have not adapted to the "style" of *The New Yorker*; rather, each of them, like Gretchen Simpson, has enlarged its dimensions. The styles, from that of Rea Irvin, who did the first cover, in February, 1925 – the symbolic Eustace Tilley, which is reprinted each year on the magazine's anniversary – through those of William Cotton, Mary Petty, Helen Hokinson, Saul Steinberg, Charles Martin, and Ed Koren, are as different as any that works of art can embody, yet the spirit of all is unmistakably *New Yorker*, because that spirit is a composite of their work.

Those who are not familiar with the mechanics of publishing a magazine may not realize that covers (except for news weeklies) are scheduled and engraved many weeks ahead of publication. In addition, *The New Yorker* maintains a "bank" of finished covers for future use. Covers with an element of immediacy are rare, although many are seasonal, as this collection has been structured to show. There is no formal deadline. While I was attending a Presidential convention, I got an idea for a cover. It seemed so right that I did it as soon as I got home, and rushed it to the magazine. The editors liked it and bought it. It was published four years later.

To the editors, there are no classifications of cover content, but one finds that the covers fall into two general groups: One consists of what Alan Dunn called "comment art," and the other is made up of work that is more subjective. To Dunn, comment art is a statement of an idea in visual form, with aesthetics not a primary concern. This surely could not be the interpretation of Mary Petty (Mrs. Alan Dunn), whose enchanting comments, on which she labored long and lovingly, are among the most aesthetically satisfying of all *New Yorker* covers. Or of Edna Eicke: a comment artist, certainly, but very much a painter. To Peter Arno, perhaps the boldest poster artist in the group, the most important point was the interdependence of idea and picture, and to Arno the picture came first. He was known to draw dozens of versions of his works over forty-hour stretches before he was satisfied. For Steinberg, comment art is more a cerebral exercise, frequently approaching the abstract. He is delighted to be asked what one of his pictures "means," and invariably refuses to explain. He does explain, though, that his great obsession is with the magic of line — with manipulating the simple pen line into sometimes conflicting definitions of space and thought. Among the subjective artists I include Ilonka Karasz, Arthur Getz, and Charles Martin. Their covers are more observations than "ideas," and there is less to study in the content. They are, simply, beautiful. And so I return to Steig, whose covers are both subjective *and* comment art. During the more than fifty years of his enormous productivity, Steig has evolved through more personal styles than one can count, becoming more and more childlike in technique and more and more complex in content. Within his direct statements he demonstrates a fundamental quality of all great graphic art: grace. It is there in Thurber, Karasz, John Held, Jr., Addams, and Alajalov.

I must say I regret the fact that some of *The New Yorker*'s greatest cartoonists never did covers: Carl Rose, Sam Cobean, Richard Taylor. Whitney Darrow, Jr., did only two, George Price only one. Perhaps they were

I

REA IRVIN
February 21, 1925
Gouache
$17\frac{1}{2} \times 13\frac{1}{4}$ in.

Rea Irvin's drawing of a Regency dandy appeared
on the cover of the first issue of *The New Yorker*.
It has reappeared every year since, on the issue closest
to the date of the original February 21, 1925 issue.
Mr. Irvin also designed *The New Yorker* logotype
as used on the magazine's cover.

remembering the answer that Harold Ross gave when he was asked why he didn't start publishing the cartoons in color. Ross said, "What's funny about red?"

One cover artist was color-blind. Perry Barlow always cleared the colors with his wife.

And one other delightful piece of *New Yorker* history: Look up the April 23, 1932, issue, and you'll find a cover of a sea horse wearing a feed bag. It was done by E. B. White.

It is not cult worship to say that many *New Yorker* covers stand among the finest works in American art over these sixty years. Art critics traditionally dismiss so-called commercial art as a stepchild of fine art, focussing their fond attention (for or against) on what they consider pure creativity. Without mounting a major attack, I would like to point out that from cave drawings through the Minoan, Egyptian, Greek, and Renaissance periods (to name a few) art was the product of artists working on commissions of one form or another. I look forward to the day when a good number of the works in this exhibition find their way into major museums, as they already have into distinguished private collections all over the world. Today, the Nicholls Gallery specializes in the original work of *New Yorker* artists; other artists are represented individually.

Seeing one's work on the cover of *The New Yorker* is a heady feeling, I can tell you. (Just laying the logotype over the top of a drawing suddenly gives it an elegant look.) It remains the daydream of many otherwise successful and famous artists — more than would admit to it. Some people sell a single cover and redirect their lives as future *New Yorker* regulars only to find that one cover is all they can do. Some regulars stop in mid-career. Daniel Alain pulled up stakes and went back to France. Edna Eicke just stopped. Some years later, she got a phone call from an agency art director asking if she'd do an ad "like one of your *New Yorker* covers." "If I could do one of my *New Yorker* covers," she said, "I'd do it for *The New Yorker*."

Like all creative people, *New Yorker* regulars live in dread that the well is running dry. But somehow there is more churning down there, and — more important — new wells are bubbling into life all the time. And *The New Yorker* continues to appear week after week with bright, fresh talent gracing its covers.   — CHARLES SAXON

THE NEW YORKER

Spring

2

Edna Eicke
March 1, 1952
Casein tempera
$17\frac{5}{8} \times 12\frac{1}{4}$ in.

3

EUGÈNE MIHAESCO
March 10, 1980
Watercolor
$11\frac{7}{8} \times 8\frac{5}{8}$ in.

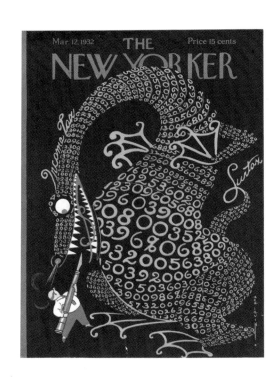

4

REA IRVIN
March 12, 1932
Watercolor, ink
$15 \times 10\frac{1}{4}$ in.

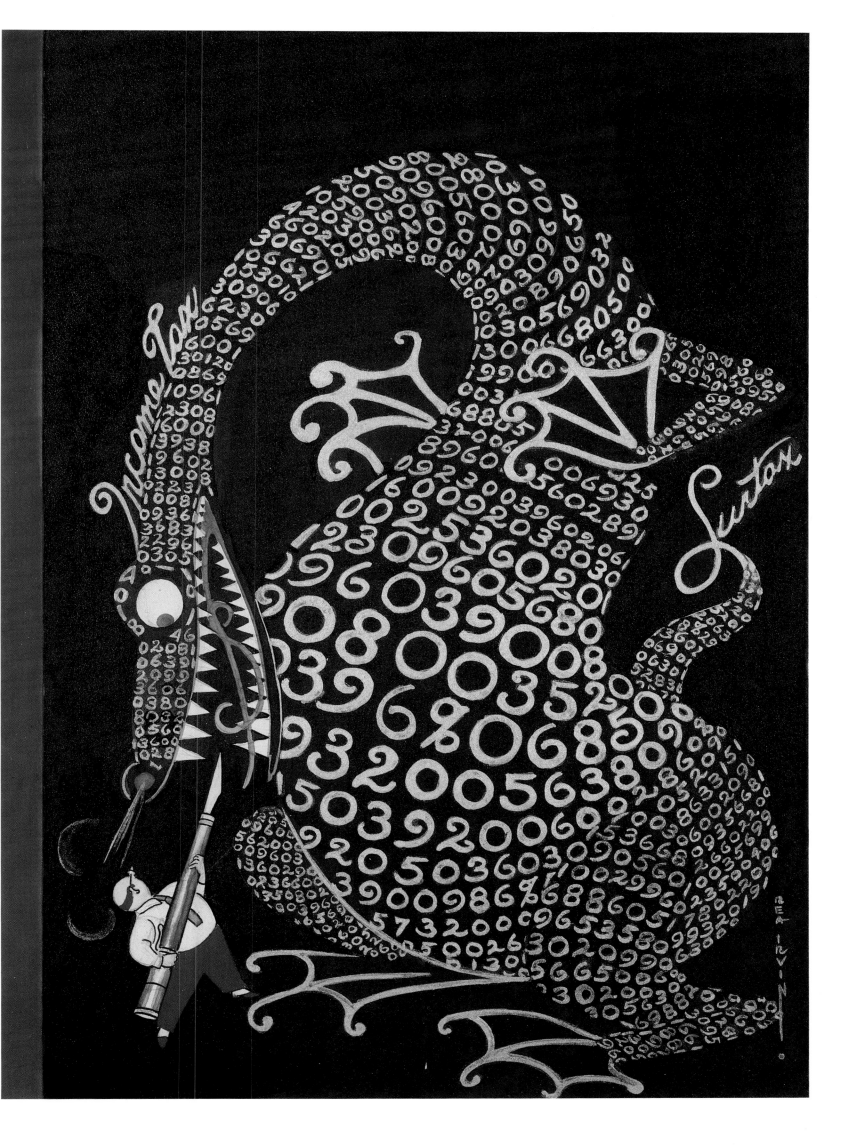

5

CHARLES MARTIN
March 18, 1972
Watercolor, pastel
$18 \times 12\frac{3}{4}$ in.

6

ARTHUR GETZ
March 22, 1958
Casein
24 × 18 in.

7

WILLIAM COTTON
March 23, 1940
Pastel
$14\frac{1}{2} \times 10\frac{1}{2}$ in.

8

CHARLES ADDAMS
March 28, 1959
Watercolor
$17\frac{1}{4} \times 11\frac{7}{8}$ in.

9

JAMES STEVENSON
April 1, 1972
Watercolor
$22\frac{3}{4} \times 17\frac{3}{8}$ in.

10

Charles Addams
April 15, 1974
Watercolor
$15\frac{1}{2} \times 11$ in.

II

PETER ARNO
April 11, 1931
Watercolor
$17 \times 12\frac{3}{4}$ in.

12

ILONKA KARASZ
May 19, 1928
Watercolor, gouache, pencil
$15\frac{5}{8} \times 11\frac{9}{16}$ in.

13

CHARLES MARTIN
June 6, 1964
Watercolor, ink, collage, acetate overlay
$13\frac{3}{4} \times 9\frac{1}{2}$ in.

14

Susan Davis
June 13, 1983
Watercolor
$22\frac{1}{2} \times 15$ in.

15

HELEN HOKINSON
June 14, 1930
Watercolor
$11\frac{1}{4} \times 8\frac{1}{16}$ in.

16

Peter Arno
June 16, 1956
Watercolor
$16\frac{1}{2} \times 12$ in.

17

GARRETT PRICE
June 25, 1949
Watercolor, pastel
$11\frac{7}{16} \times 8\frac{7}{16}$ in.

Summer

18

James Stevenson
July 1, 1972
Watercolor, pencil, collage
$11\frac{1}{2} \times 8\frac{1}{2}$ in.

19

WILLIAM COTTON
July 8, 1933
Pastel
$15 \times 11\frac{1}{8}$ in.

20

MARY PETTY
July 10, 1954
Watercolor, ink
$16\frac{15}{16} \times 11\frac{1}{8}$ in.

2 1

ANDRÉ FRANÇOIS
July 10, 1965
Gouache
$13\frac{13}{16} \times 9\frac{7}{8}$ in.

22

MARY PETTY
July 14, 1956
Watercolor, ink
$16\frac{15}{16} \times 11\frac{3}{8}$ in.

23

HELEN HOKINSON
July 26, 1930
Watercolor
12 × 9 in.

24

WILLIAM STEIG
July 28, 1975
Watercolor, ink
$10\frac{11}{16} \times 7\frac{7}{8}$ in.

For Joyce
W. Skig

25

ILONKA KARASZ
July 30, 1932
Watercolor
$15\frac{3}{8} \times 11\frac{7}{16}$ in.

26

EDNA EICKE
July 31, 1954
Casein tempera
$15\frac{5}{8} \times 10\frac{1}{16}$ in.

EDNA EICKE

27

ANATOL KOVARSKY
August 2, 1969
Tempera, ink
$26 \times 18\frac{3}{8}$ in.

28

Charles Martin
August 4, 1951
Watercolor, gouache
$17\frac{1}{2} \times 12\frac{7}{8}$ in.

29

CHARLES SAXON
August 11, 1980
Watercolor, charcoal
$16\frac{13}{16} \times 13\frac{1}{2}$ in.

30

HELEN HOKINSON
August 12, 1933
Watercolor
$11\frac{1}{4} \times 8\frac{1}{16}$ in.

3I

MARY PETTY
August 16, 1941
Watercolor, ink
$16\frac{15}{16} \times 11\frac{3}{16}$ in.

32

ABE BIRNBAUM
August 22, 1964
Gouache
$16\frac{1}{2} \times 13\frac{1}{4}$ in.

33

GRETCHEN DOW SIMPSON
August 22, 1977
Acrylic, ink
24 × 18 in.

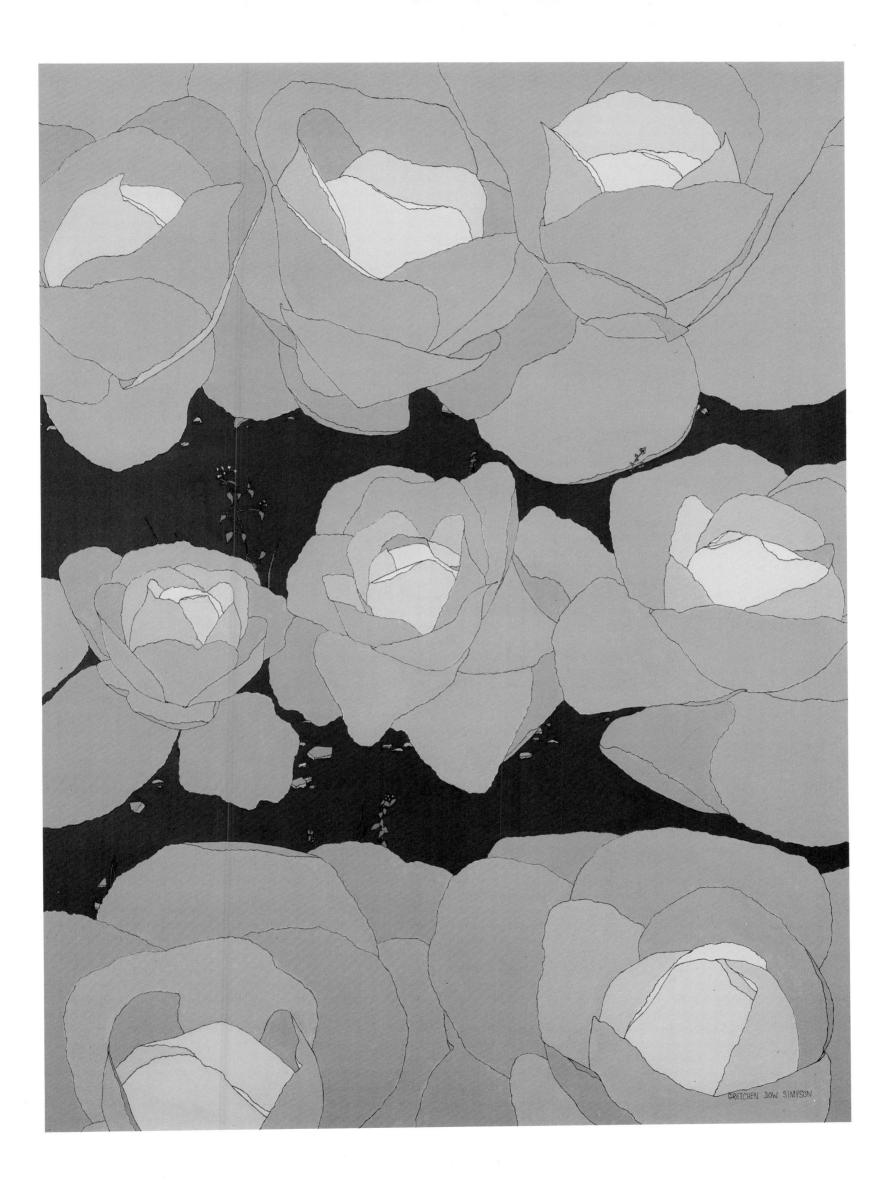

GRETCHEN DOW SIMPSON

34

EDWARD KOREN
August 28, 1971
Watercolor, India ink
$14\frac{3}{8} \times 10\frac{1}{2}$ in.

35

CONSTANTIN ALAJALOV
August 29, 1953
Mixed media
$17\frac{1}{2} \times 11\frac{13}{16}$ in.

36

LAURA JEAN ALLEN
September 2, 1967
Mixed media
$17 \times 12\frac{1}{2}$ in.

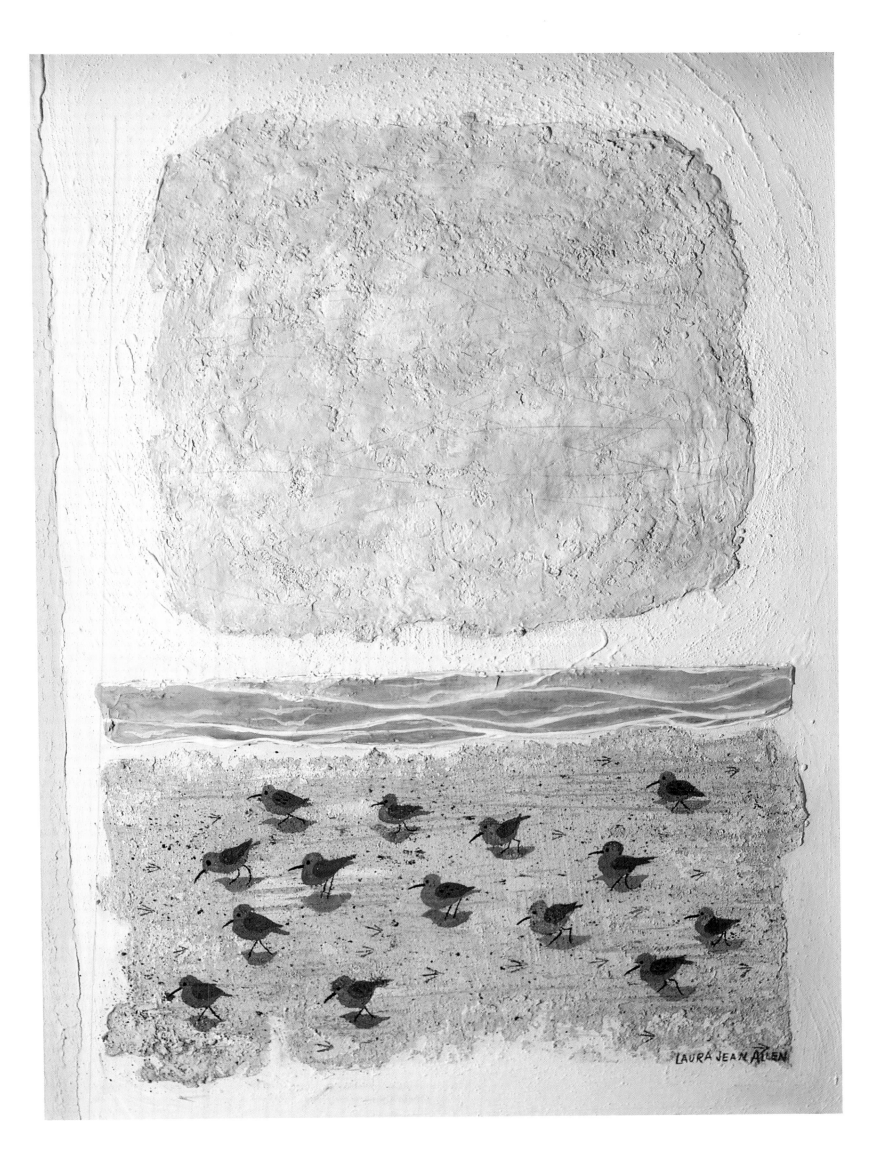

37

CHARLES SAXON
September 2, 1972
Watercolor, charcoal
$16\frac{3}{8} \times 11\frac{5}{16}$ in.

Autumn

38

ILONKA KARASZ
September 20, 1947
Gouache
$16\frac{1}{2} \times 12$ in.

39

J. C. Suarès
September 23, 1974
Watercolor, ink
$11\frac{5}{8} \times 8\frac{1}{2}$ in.

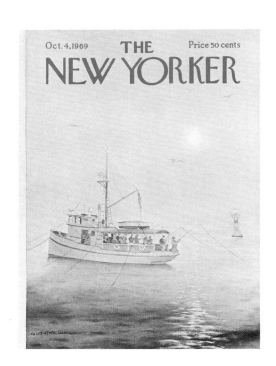

40

ALBERT HUBBELL
October 4, 1969
Watercolor
$15\frac{1}{2} \times 13\frac{1}{4}$ in.

41

CHARLES SAXON
October 7, 1974
Watercolor, ink
$14\frac{3}{8} \times 10$ in.

42

LUDWIG BEMELMANS
October 9, 1954
Gouache
$27\frac{1}{4} \times 21\frac{1}{8}$ in.

43

GRETCHEN DOW SIMPSON
October 11, 1976
Acrylic, ink
$19\frac{3}{16} \times 14$ in

GRETCHEN DOW SIMPSON

44

Perry Barlow
October 17, 1953
Watercolor, charcoal, pencil
$16\frac{7}{16} \times 12\frac{1}{8}$ in.

45

ARNIE LEVIN
October 22, 1979
Ink, wash
$9\frac{1}{2} \times 7\frac{3}{4}$ in.

46

J. J. SEMPÉ
October 25, 1982
Watercolor, ink
$22\frac{7}{16} \times 15\frac{3}{4}$ in.

47

CONSTANTIN ALAJALOV
October 28, 1939
Watercolor
$13\frac{1}{4} \times 9\frac{5}{16}$ in.

48

CHARLES MARTIN
October 28, 1974
Watercolor, acrylic
$16\frac{15}{16} \times 12$ in.

49

WILLIAM STEIG
October 31, 1959
Watercolor, ink
$12\frac{1}{16} \times 9$ in.

50

CHARLES ADDAMS
October 31, 1983
Watercolor, ink
$17\frac{1}{4} \times 12\frac{1}{4}$ in.

51

JAMES STEVENSON
November 4, 1974
Watercolor, pencil
$23\frac{13}{16} \times 16\frac{1}{16}$ in.

52

RONALD SEARLE
November 8, 1969
Watercolor, ink, crayon
$14\frac{3}{4} \times 10\frac{1}{16}$ in.

53

PETER ARNO
November 17, 1951
Watercolor
$17\frac{1}{2} \times 12$ in.

54

ILONKA KARASZ
November 23, 1963
Watercolor
$16 \times 10\frac{3}{4}$ in.

55

ARTHUR GETZ
November 17, 1956
Gouache
$23\frac{15}{16} \times 18\frac{1}{16}$ in.

56

SAUL STEINBERG
November 29, 1976
Colored pencil, ink
$23 \times 14\frac{1}{2}$ in.

STEINBERG
1976

57

ROBERT KRAUS
November 30, 1957
Mixed media
$15\frac{1}{2} \times 11\frac{1}{16}$ in.

Winter

58

CHARLES SAXON
December 16, 1967
Watercolor, charcoal
14 × 10 in.

59

JEAN MICHEL FOLON
December 17, 1973
Watercolor
$11\frac{7}{8} \times 8\frac{7}{8}$ in.

60

61

André François
December 23, 1972
Gouache
$16\frac{3}{4} \times 12\frac{3}{16}$ in.

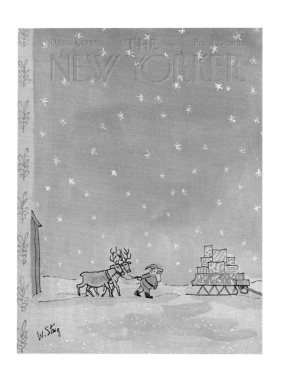

62

WILLIAM STEIG
December 24, 1966
Watercolor, gouache, ink
$12\frac{5}{16} \times 9$ in.

63

GEORGE PRICE
December 25, 1965
Watercolor
$15\frac{7}{8} \times 11\frac{1}{8}$ in.

64

Jenni Oliver

65

PERRY BARLOW
December 28, 1940
Watercolor, ink, pencil
$16\frac{7}{8} \times 11\frac{9}{16}$ in.

66

CHARLES MARTIN
December 30, 1972
Watercolor
$17\frac{11}{16} \times 12\frac{5}{16}$ in.

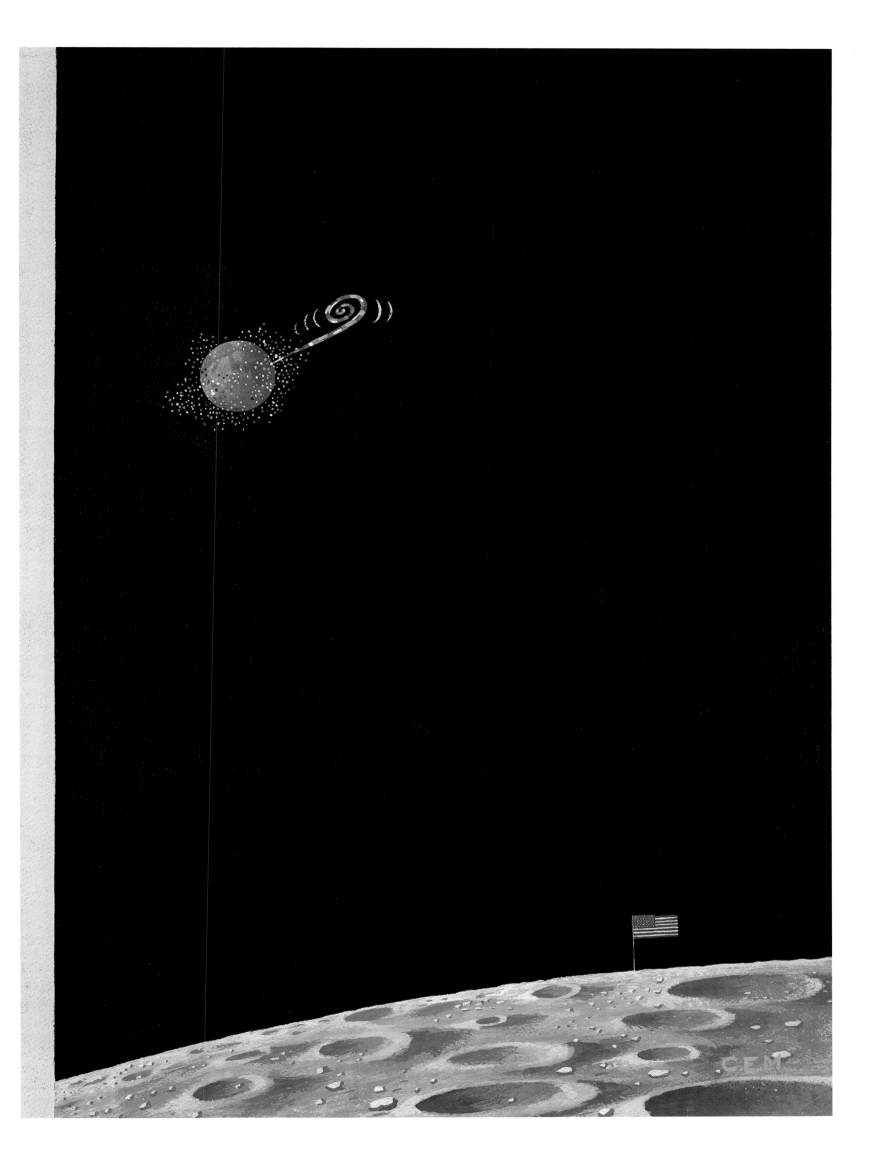

67

CHARLES SAXON
January 15, 1972
Watercolor, charcoal
$13\frac{9}{16} \times 10$ in.

68

SAUL STEINBERG
January 16, 1965
Mixed media
$22 \times 14\frac{1}{2}$ in.

Florida

STEINBERG

69

Constantin Alajalov
January 18, 1958
Watercolor, ink
$18\frac{3}{4} \times 14\frac{3}{4}$ in.

70

GARRETT PRICE
January 25, 1964
Acrylic
$14\frac{1}{2} \times 9\frac{3}{4}$ in.

71

PETER ARNO
January 28, 1956
Watercolor
$16\frac{1}{8} \times 11\frac{13}{16}$ in.

72

ILONKA KARASZ
January 29, 1927
Watercolor
$15\frac{1}{2} \times 12$ in.

73

WILLIAM COTTON
February 9, 1935
Pastel
14 × 10 in.

74

CHARLES ADDAMS
February 10, 1951
Watercolor
$11\frac{5}{8} \times 7\frac{7}{8}$ in.

75

André François
February 17, 1975
Pastel, ink
$13\frac{3}{8} \times 10\frac{1}{4}$ in.

76

PERRY BARLOW
February 12, 1955
Watercolor, ink, pencil
$16 \times 11\frac{1}{2}$ in.

77

Abe Birnbaum
February 14, 1948
Mixed media
$14\frac{1}{2} \times 10\frac{1}{2}$ in.

78

PETER ARNO
February 15, 1930
Watercolor, ink, crayon
$16\frac{1}{2} \times 12$ in.

79

WILLIAM COTTON
February 21, 1948
Watercolor, pastel
14 × 10 in.

Feb. 28, 1970 THE Price 50 cents
NEW YORKER

80

JAMES STEVENSON
February 28, 1970
Collage
23 × 19 in.

ARTIST INDEX